**BOA**
EDITIONS LTD

# Seasons of Lotus, Seasons of Bone

# Seasons of Lotus, Seasons of Bone

—

Poems by
MATTHEW SHENODA

American Poets Continuum Series, No. 118

—

BOA Editions, Ltd. – Rochester, N.Y. – 2009

First Edition
09 10 11 12 7 6 5 4 3 2 1

For information about permission to reuse any material from this book please
contact The Permissions Company at www.permissionscompany.com or e-mail
permdude@eclipse.net.

Publications by BOA Editions, Ltd. – a not-for-profit corporation under section
501 (c) (3) of the United States Internal Revenue Code – are made possible
with funds from a variety of sources, including public funds from the New York
State Council on the Arts, a state agency; the Literature Program of the National
Endowment for the Arts; the County of Monroe, NY; the Lannan Foundation
for support of the Lannan Translations Selection Series; the Sonia Raiziss Giop
Charitable Foundation; the Mary S. Mulligan Charitable Trust; the Rochester Area
Community Foundation; the Arts & Cultural Council for Greater Rochester; the
Steeple-Jack Fund; the Ames-Amzalak Memorial Trust in memory of Henry Ames,
Semon Amzalak and Dan Amzalak; and contributions from many individuals
nationwide.

See Colophon on page 88 for special individual acknowledgements.

Cover Design: Daphne Morrissey
Cover Art: "House of Sheba" by Wosene Worke Kosrof
Interior Design and Composition: Bill Jones
Manufacturing: BookMobile
BOA Logo: Mirko

Library of Congress Cataloging-in-Publication Data

Shenoda, Matthew.
Seasons of lotus, seasons of bone / by Matthew Shenoda. -- 1st ed.
    p.cm.
ISBN 978-1-934414-27-9 (alk. paper)
1. Egypt--Poetry. I. Title.

PS3619.H4538S43 2009
811'.6--dc22

                                    2009016967

NATIONAL
ENDOWMENT
FOR THE ARTS
A great nation
deserves great art.

BOA Editions, Ltd.
Nora A. Jones, Executive Director/Publisher
Thom Ward, Editor/Production
Peter Conners, Editor/Marketing
Bernadette Catalana, BOA Board Chair
A. Poulin, Jr., Founder (1938-1996)
250 North Goodman Street, Suite 306
Rochester, NY 14607
www.boaeditions.org

State of the Arts
NYSCA

*In Memory of Abuna Antonious Henein*
    My map from this life to the next.


*for Christina*
    My unabridged spirit.


*and for Makarios*
    In hope these words may help you to remember.

# CONTENTS

## I. Songs of the Lost Days

## II. Songs of Tainted Waters

# I. Songs of the Lost Days

*A child is born in this world*
*He needs protection*
*God, guide and protect us*
*When we're wrong correct us*

*And stand by me*
*In high seas or in low seas*

– Bob Marley, "High Tide or Low Tide"

# Schism

One man dreams
Of fire
But cannot strike
Two sticks

Together

One man strikes
Two sticks
But cannot dream
Of fire

# Donkey Carts and Desolation

Dilapidated clapboard shacks
piles of bricks in the sand
scratching at the surface of cohesion

Ingenuity is the notion of building
On a foundation made from loss

Out in these arid expanses
where the Red Sea meets the sand
people dream of progress
made from humility
and the laughter of others
multi-colored dross scatters the earth
like foreign shrubbery

We converse in codes of motion
Language signaling daily headway

Advice for the long haul.

# Apparition

Leaving delineation
she walks with lineal light
where understanding of fingertips
and vision are what reign

A halo effect on the skyline
Linking one age to another
Manetho prayed for past

& the children
exiled from their nature
made to run through
the tenements of history
broken in syncopated time
driven by the music
of forgetfulness
rising from rupture
of wheat fields
will sing, a rekhyt unfurled
ushering in, a new song

# Season of Lotus

This age, no longer about invention
Steadfast–tradition

When the sun sets
West–death

We guard ourselves from its evanescent light
Concentrate east

Ask protection–thrice
Know that our language will soon be a ghost

Each stone hewed in perpendicular time
We face the sea

Give thanks for the smooth and rough of our hands
Thread silk through our crania and glitter

Knowing that we can glitter like morning tide
Knowing the sun will never set

Death will never hold
Glittering–resurrection

We know no other way
Need not to

We have done it this way
As long as the river

We began our lives
Like this, in glitter

In this
The season of lotus

# Miracle Song

The communal body
pregnant with hope
etched with Nile tributaries
guarded by wrought iron lotus
fetching water from pools of desire.

Belief is strewn on the cane horizon
dripping with a yearning for truth.
We have known of this other world so long
surely Shenu is not lost
what stands before us cannot be.

Every stone stacked in vain?

*Oh Lord, I'm your weary child*
*give me a sign.*

Your power belongs to us
we are your wayward vision
make the light to shine through our dome.

Make this life worthy of the next
split the sea of heart & mind
make us to remember our forgetfulness.

*Lord, I'm your weary child.*

Paint our faces in your light
our wrists in your sign
let them know, it is us.

*Lord, I am a raven with bread.*

Surely it is us
if ever there was a code to decipher
we are your key.

*Lord, my roots sprout three trunks.*

*Lord, I am a rock made of wheat.*

# Countryside

Why toss a bird in the sky
& not allow her to fly?

　　Cane juice flows
　　& palm leaves eddy
　　in the heart of a heart
　　the place where songs are made from stone

Why split the fusion
& make a box for two?

　　Let the thatch roof dry
　　this is the place of hasad
　　where rebel communities anchor
　　their fists in land

Why create clash
& call it natural?

　　Let the hills roll
　　& the seeds resist the cover of soil
　　this is the storm that feeds
　　the place of compressed, rural strength

Why breathe fire
& call it light?

　　Let the hands cup rain
　　& the feet wade
　　these are the kamanga strings
　　that bend for humanity

Why try to confound the spirit
when the spirit's greater than you?

    Let us be hibiscus flower
    & let the people go where they need to go
    along the road paved with cane
    & double binds

# Entrance

I have learned that script, like sky
    contains no end.

Words can create saplings
    sprouting from the line of your lips.

I have learned that words, like smoke
    rise from this earth
    & return again
like currents.

I have learned that faces
    give record
    often articulated
by the creases of another man's face.

# for our Grandmothers

*for Tata Fawziyya*

You are the last one
Having emptied yourself from the world
You are the last one

Countries border countries
But in the grooves of our hands
We understand only the touch of rivers and seas
We turn ourselves inside out and walk through
Military checkpoints and police barricades
Airport securities and bus lines
We turn ourselves inside out
over and over
to reach our loved ones

each trip to see you became more polluted
diesel fumes consuming the road from Cairo
but the delta never lost its green
never lost its twisted vines
and the people continue despite the greatest efforts
to stop them
you continued       like the ancient mausoleums
beside the road to you, honoring our ancestry
you continued
until your grandchildren were grown
with trans-Atlantic prayers
we battled our youth in plastic land
spinning our fists into tarot root
praying:

*Raise the Nile to its measures*
*according to Your grace*

*Give joy to the face of the earth*
*May its furrows be abundantly watered*
*Its fruits be plentiful*
*Prepare the land for sowing and harvesting...*

keeping safe our lineage in the limestone rock
we've used to find our past
we are memory-seekers
buried in diasporic silt

some may say that any street will do
but the air here is different
no matter how clean        no matter
it's an earthless air
blowing without direction
without a word to guide it

# In This Place

From the air, you understand
topography is a child's feet
dragging through sand.

The coral heads of the Red Sea
dotting a map from Africa
to the Levant.

In between, the sea and the rise of Sinai,
the Nile, and the streets of Cairo,
the air hangs heavy with trepidation
calling for the weaver to save the sky
with cotton yarn and indigo dye.

We promise ourselves that this world will sustain us
that the spring will not dry before our children's thirst.

We run our fingers on sandstone
speak stories in rivets and impressions.

We cup our hands for water
and pray the birds will learn to drink.

The architecture of the streets we rise from
is shaped from fragility and resilience.

The peddler's kufiyah woven with understanding
wind can kill or save in this desert.

Beneath the scarves which cover these furrows
lives colored by the farmer's plow.

We wonder why the children's eyes have grown so large—
igniting this charcoal landscape.

# Road to al-Qahira

in memory, Cairo is a pomegranate
born of the fertility that bursts from her river

her streets glow like marrow in bone
shaped from fragments

frayed with the grit of time
aged is her heart

alleys that ache with empty bellies
and smile with eyes carved from sandstone

God bless the city
and the children in her breast

torsos wrapped in cloth
no telling what kind of song their chests sing

expanding like the ribs of your swollen wrists
we don't speak these things

they exist
like a tree gnarled by wind

when people rise from where they stand
stretch themselves closer to sky

they begin to see things from another angle
water becomes stone, water becomes light

on these streets
a spirit made of human thread

learns to pull apart the past
and watch it flower in sand

only then will we cut something green
only then will we cut something fresh

# Movement

Twisting from one topography to another
we understand movement through waves
& curves.

Wind & water
begin to stretch us
across microclimates
and make bridges out of bodies.

Ancestry is a shuffling
from one crease to another
a siren that calls through space
shedding its decibels
& shaping orbs in the atmosphere of the past.

Connection is the ardor
that two things can come together
that space can be shared by time.

Loss is the shifting and (re)formation
of expansions created from dust...

Tension is the sense
that things are determined
by something greater than you.

Movement is the muscle
that guides the clouds
and makes space for rain.

# Veranda Views

The land has been dissolved
Only the spirit of the people remains

Sitting on the concrete veranda
Kinky haired boys are strumming up a street corner game

Winding through city hills where young boys kick balls in
    alley ways
Dusted out in their best school clothes
They shake linguistic dice and straddle themselves on the iron
    rod barrier
The cage that keeps them in this city
Concrete stained like charred corn

Because what we've seen is not enough
In a world of compact dispersion
Weeds squeeze through sidewalk cracks like fists breaking air

Follow me through this winding alley into the sharp crumbling
    plaster of old women's memories
Break this water into fragments
And follow me into the belly of this city's beast
Where young girls scrawl their dreams into dirt like concrete
    calligraphy

Wrought ironed dreams end in sharp points
Where I stand, fingers wrapped around the gates, pulling from
    memory

Some children are born from the rhythm of Algeria
Some of them the daughters of Egypt's song

Reed-reading black eyes colored by river sediment
Drunk on boza that seeps from a nova

Shuffling to dips and grooves like coral membrane

# In the Season of Paremhat

There is too much talk
Forgetting to watch
The river split
We seek to understand
The delta which makes our humanity
Tangible
Our hands fork silt
To make music

Music is the way we forget to talk
We say, music is the way we forget to talk

The hand bends with goat skin

Making a palm drum speak for the future
hope of resistance in the taut skin

Farmer to drum
Farmer to drum
Farmer to drum

One long gallabiyya
On the horizon etched into eternity by a river of
    understanding

Women of wheat
Women of wheat
Kneel near the bank for understanding

Oh, hear us in our invocation
Let us be known through our greetings

The body begins to acquiesce beneath the midday sunlight

Allah
Allah
Allah

The body begins to spiral to earth

# Brotherhood

somewhere between the buzzing telephone wires of a city on
    fire
and the mirage of water reflected in skulls

the recall of wheels spinning on a looming earth
oud strings echo from side to side to make this space

and to you my brothers
a song
from the heart
not written on the pages of history
or currency
but buried in the rock of our brotherhood
unearthed by a force
given us this time
by elders who call for us to rise
and ask that we carry their spirits
in being
men
the men we were taught to be
by the world behind us
by the shore that has lead us into memory

*remember*

there is a balance between the eyes
a steadiness in each foot
a calm at our napes that the lyncher cannot see
there is a memory lodged in our biceps
teaching us with each flex
we can breathe fire
through our widened chests
and exhale       cool
wind

*remember*

My brothers
You are either of river
or sea
silt
or salt

the strange fruit dripping from a tree
wet skin slick like blood puddle
in a city not theirs to name
African memory = rope

If the cage is made of corrugated steel
what then do we make of our freedom?

*remember*

our hearts beyond the shanty town
our spirits free of this place
proof that we never die

never

die

never die

# From Scetis to Sohag

## I

make my face to be like sand
history leaking between brick & mortar
an effervescence of earth
windows of Baramos
shutters of sweeping sky

## II

we move across Atlantic schism
sail the memory of the forgotten
shed our feet
to touch rock
in this our ancestral home

## III

to Him that divided the Red Sea into parts
an inheritance
outstretched in this heat.
Creator, make me a gazelle who
roams these cliffs an eternity

## IV

spin the wheat of our sustenance
rejoice in this toil
orbit the planet of palm and date
set free the tongue of want
grind, revolution, grind

## V

on the mount of Ansina
I speak green across the valley
each word a prayer
psalm-memory deep within this rock
revelation seekers

## VI

by the staff of my elders
I will walk in the line
that they have walked
unlock the gaze from beneath my tomb
& rise like frankincense

## VII

and what if we were a cavalcade
into eternity
steer our mules into eternal pastures
take with us nothing more
than color and faith?

## VIII

Dayr al-Barsha
painted like marrow & bone
each line a symphonic everlasting
unfurling the wings of the rekhyt
so that we may enter like lotus

## IX

falcon became raven
anubis–lion
my elders, open armed in habitation
make yourselves of this place
so as never to remain here

## X

etched on the surface of our village
a marker of our existence
dry hooks colored with the past
rising with childhood dreams
beyond any affliction

## XI

in this byword world
we rise to the taste of salt
make edible our seeds
and cover the village
with our half-eaten shells

## XII

can we read papyrus in neon
understand our course by way of this
foreign illumination
compressed under night sky
by this, the only river's edge?

## XIII

peace must come before the name
find the swelling in the river of your spine
learn to read the eyes of another
this modern hieroglyphics
this modern day tome

## XIV

we learn our names by water
blessed in the river of struggle
and from beneath the dome, recount:
*mubarak al-ati bism al-Rubb*
*mubarak al-ati bism al-Rubb*

## XV

wondrous is your song
dusk-chant
rippling through the palm fronds
awaiting
eastern resurrection

## for Mesopotamia

submerged in the lines of your brow
the Tigris begins her journey
a river yearning for immunity
in this Mesopotamia, this "Land between the Rivers"
Dijla runs eastward inside of you
river of Eden
unable to annunciate the letter that begins prisons
free to meander and find your ancestral home
to long for your ancient lover Hapi
as the Tigris winds through your two halves
she continues her journey like the lines of your eyes
trailing charcoal in the evening of your lips
her creases free to emanate
like the curves of your breasts
rich in abundance
open to the ability of emergence
yearning for the sea inside of you
and on this night Hapi dreams of you
near grass-seeded earth
he reaches for you
as the crocodile's paddle sends ripples
expanding infinitely
until swallowed by your breath...

# Oasis

it is not enough to lament
to acquiesce to the bordered divisions of country

only once in a person's life
can the sun become perfectly whole

imbedded at the nape
reminiscent of home

all other moments
are those of simple humanity

cacophonous tapestries
of sun & cloud, sea & river

for a wanderer to savor
for an artist to breathe

here in this scorching sun
a signal towards life

beyond a road sign
or a finely finished chair

beyond the temple of a windstorm
inside the gliding stone of remembrance

beyond a box of ivory or wood
despite cowry adornment

a lover stands bare in this desert
facing her lover

offering only the sweat
from the small of her back

# Night Song

let it be night
that the arrows of day be shadowed
& the almond candle of your eyes

shine night
read every word / honey on the wound
let it be day

in the open river
that mountain goat may step to rock
like I step to you

rock of ages
psalm song / palm line
water curl

I give myself to this word
commit to eternity
traced by slender shadows / ask for nothing

still riddled by the bullets
of Mogadishu / Darfur / distance
political bombast

the son of diaspora
learns to live in shade
without the battle of journey / graze slender

we make ourselves heart-travelers
live near water
& find the longest star

if there is beauty here
we drink it / mouth full of sand
& on the silt of our tongues

comes the tree of words
blossoming into breath
*paradise*

# II. Songs of Tainted Waters

*Well what we know*
*Is not what they tell us*
*We're not ignorant, I mean it*
*And they just cannot touch us*
*Through the powers of the Most High*
*We keep on surfacing*
*Through the powers of the Most High*
*We keep on surviving*

   – Bob Marley, "Ambush In the Night"

# A Note Found in the Tomb of Tutankhamen

*for the British Museum*

Possessor / ignorant of the converse

One geology / cancel another
One past / haunt another

You who does not understand that our speech is prayer

*When every arrow of my body*
*Shoots towards heaven*
*The hieroglyph of my spine*
*Made run through my front*

Shattered in the folds of my hand
A young boy I was
Rested to this place to be one with Ra

They took me to the valley at Thebes
Peace my soul from tomb robbers

Hidden / eternity
Sealed with the doctrine of eternal existence

Now you have unsettled the cataract of the Nile
And disturbed the very sun that shields you

Hard-headed Brit
Did five attempts to steal me not warn you
White man / always to himself a hero
Howard Carter / tomb robber
Take the sterling from your Lord Carnarvon
You cannot buy yourself eternity

This life was never material

Who believes / believes
Impotent in your knowledge          beast
Grave robber / blinded by primitive massacre
Unable to not know how

Why was never enough.

Unbeliever!

Alive in my death mask
Eternally a cobra
I am become my own protector
What am I to do in these strange times
3000 years I lay whole
Shrouded in my new name
Lay distant from the heresy
And you who unwrap me
Make my bones degenerate
For a glimpse / think yourself worthy of my touch

Unable to embrace mystery.
I sing the song chorused by palm fronds in wind
You have missed the message

You have not seen everlasting.

# Mummified

Marry emotion to intellect

The human heart
Removed

The brain
Removed

Mummified

In the arch of a tomb

Mummified

In the wraps of a spine

Mummified

In the etching of gold

Mummified

In the breath of an open hand
Where sky can disappear water
Disappear day
& make night in the heat of your palm

Intentional preservation
Obsessed with the obelisk of after-life

A symbol contained for what cannot
Be held

One by one

Mummified

In service to Ra

Sun can rise
So can insan

Illuminated by vision

Mummified

Not for the preservation of earth
Not for the preservation of bone

Carry us beyond the wind
Into the spiral of an eye

We were beckoned in unison

Beyond the wreck of survival

We were made to think

Who can understand this deviation
Where the mind becomes a mummy

Leaders call for material ascendancy

Empire, an ego

No vision for the far side

And so they cross the sea to thieve our insides
Make themselves whole with a refuse organ

Remember Kom Ombo
Remember the rekyht
Symbol of the captives we've become

Papyrus of Ani
Spoke nothing of this earth

The land was a path to the heavens
The river
Between cataracts
Now a barrier
Severing life from life

# Cityscape

the trees speak paramour in rapid light

children milk industrial utters
seeping urethane strychnine and cracked moon-beams

sidewalk cracks play
shadow dances

garbage collectors rock the night

third world meals are consumed by consumption
telephone lines buzz hymns to bigger bread

dancing ska makes us forget maggot images

mystery is an elephant with tusks made of bamboo poles

fantasy is a world where we're alright

corner store shop clerks send blessings through vegetables
while war rages beneath the counter

we lay brick in circles and wonder why we're trapped

my city was built with an armada gate
hinges rusted by expired dreams

God bless the garbage collectors
who hide the filth from our eyes
and allow us to live in this disillusion

one child learns to scratch the eye of another
save her from the horizon

immigrants wring the necks of ducks
and privilege pays to sue them

at the base of every city tree is a crack
waiting for lightning to break it free

oily rags are signs of survival

the sun is eclipsed by spent diapers and white pacifiers

## Voices from the Rubble

I am through with this earth
and its twisted roots
wringing our veins
the soil has molded like wheat
frosting our vision and taste
every street has run counter to our travels
our hearts have been drained into the seas.

It is time for us
to dig
unearth the earth from itself.

# Between Neighbor & Nation

Two tongues
amid chaos & stillness

It is that we have
somehow troubled our nature
in order to preserve it
and in doing so have forgotten
a piece of ourselves

    & you who wished to make this
    the center of your kingdom
    dismiss those who live on its periphery
    gaze up, wish not
    a shackled solidarity
    a stringency that snaps
    the neck of the Hudhud
    & makes bobble our daily compass

Forever an expanse
never an embrace

    the hem of the dress
    trailing, trailing
    airy in its prompting of past
    we shuffle dust between
    rock-stone & tree bark
    conceal creation in the
    cavity of our front
    & make warmth of our hands
    rough shell

& you who echo loudly
a caliphate promise

hurriedly made of slaughter & fur
bloodied with the shadow
of front-raised eyes
the refuse of your kingdom
made maligned & mute
sand made to glass once more

    An old man rubs his finger along a dusty rail
    Knows how this soil has healed generations
    Smudges his face on the horizon of his head
    & steps to the curb

When we gather together
all the kin of Gebel Barkal
those who expect
nothing less than
generational survival

    A child cups her hand in river water
    Knows too much about her history to drink

The Lions of Aker made clear our path
sunrise to sunset
in the name of the Most High
valiant survival

# Ecology

*after Mahmoud Darwish*

I dreamt of this exodus
This wrapping back into
What has been unwrapped
And again beginning to see Home

I breathe now as I've begun to resurrect

If we learn to write our memories on skin…

The half-bent sun
Tries hard to muffle cries
But sometimes
Children need to wail
Because change is hard to take

How many really understand the shifts that shape us…

Losing the earth can burn us

How many bodies feed the tree of your childhood…

How bad does the lyncher hate the earth
To turn his hands to rope?

And what of the furniture maker
Who cannot make a living
By a rocking chair
But rather by a coffin

Where does the lotus drift
When the river has been dammed for eternity

How do our children learn reed songs
When their bones are placards for plants

We walk beside the howling train
Confounded by monoxide and soil yearning to oxidize
The plastics now float like leaves
And the Ginn from deep inside the earth
Rises to taunt society,
Spewing words:
>    *Progress*
>    *Tomorrow*
>    *Progress*
>    *Tomorrow*
And your grandmother can only feel yesterday in her aching
    body
Knowing that yesterday is gone and tomorrow may never
    come

So today is just a memory of forgetfulness

# Continuance

tightly woven in the curls of her hair
the rosetta stone of tomorrow

in every sandstorm, a beginning
muscled in the tension of tides

the whirling of date palms
the journey of exchange

floating on the placid ambit of affection
each strand a key to uncover the temple of understanding

mired by the elastic expansion of dread
trembling before the altars of fear

unearthing a body from the wreck of invasion
the woman frozen, her hands, aged, reminiscent of love

learn to touch the sky like salient arrows
fierce the aftermath of desperation

she unravels her hair from beyond her
drops her curls into sunrise
levies her body towards home

crowded by the darkness of suspect
she brushes her hands to the floor
raises the grain of her wakefulness

watches the river rise green
with a smile across her brow
her eyes made of cowry and gold

she begins in the order of sunset
preparing fish for the fire
she kneads the dough of celebration

gathering kin
in the shade of acacia
she thrusts to the knee

cracks the cane
disseminates sweetness
fibrous light in their mouths

## for Lower Nubia

There was a time in this very spot
before the dam was resurrected
before the now dead president flooded a culture
when everything was black and brown.

Nubia thrived by the grace of Horus
people styled tombs.

Villages moved with the pace of elders
temples changed by time of day
everything was black and brown.

Now beneath the glimmer of a beautiful lake
relics evaporate from the surface
masks reflect in the ripples
their images stretching to the shore

and the only color left is blue.

# Recollection

what we have killed in this world
will rise up against us
grass will stage rebellions
in the shape of banana plantations
children will hold council
on the edges of garbage dumps
floating like plastic ashes

the water will overcome us
& our dignity will be perched
in the delta of mangrove branches
palm bark will cover our feet from shame

the mason has called to his children
his tile work the scales of fish

learn to shudder in this life
shake the pollen from your hair

his daughter's eyelids gnarl into finch songs
& thread water with the nurture of understanding
she stands beside her mother
conjuring dawn
they sing the songs of redemption
their verve feeding fig groves

I remember being a child
coyote hills & whitecap beaches

I remember how men swung chains
in the face of fear
trying to combat the cardamom sun

# The Cusp

If we share this humanity with one another
Is it not our place to gnarl each other's lips into utterances of
    love?
Should we not beg from our kin the calling of human
    embrace?

When the oratory of humanity
Remains on the shelf of dignity
Our hearts begin to bend in batik patterns
And the fruits of the trees scent the air beneath us

The children of starvation are calling our names
Begging of us a leaf of dignity to cover their shame

The mountains are singing with alabaster notes
Their sounds making dust on our streets

We are climbing for the hills of our ancestry
Seeking the forgiveness of the water-wheel

The dancer has entered the village in hopes of transforming
    the night
When all the children gather
She will move them away from their homes and mold them
    each into rows

olive groves with citrus soil

Whose life is present on the bureaucrats agenda?
Who will nurture dignity and watch the mist rise from the
    hills?

We have outspoken our land
And promised her to the enemy's son

Her river has increased by an abundance of waste
And all that was in her is tainted

# Remembering Zeytun

The trash crumpling on the streets
The dirt scratching to the sounds of our feet
Donkey carts clicking like birds
Songs of burning trash and exhaust fumes
That hiss like sunrise.

Tabla beats sliding out of windows
Midday gossip drifting to the streets
Lost in the shuffle of dusty soccer balls
Scraping the dirt like leaves on water
When the heat swells up we bounce from the streets
And find refuge in watermelon.

The scent of charred corn and decomposition
Evoke palm trees and singing rivers
Crumbling buildings and laughing children
Makes urban wrecks feel like progress
And shiny streets a trap.

## Season of Bone

Poverty we have seen
but never this soulless gaze
of beast and human
the trees beg their maker
for drought
unable to bear the thought
of survival
in a forgotten land

And here before the cadence of war
the screeching symphony of vile stalkers
drowned in the memory of the aggrieved
the river of his head swells and swallows
his wife and children a reverie to the rubble
lost in the crevice of the whip hand's undertaking

He prays for ascendancy,
wanders the Red Sea shore
names each fish like a child
something to bear the loss

He cries to the youth
pulls at the flesh of his eyes

We will rise from the mist of oppression
like rejuvenated reeds on the banks of the River

# On the River: A Nile Lament in Twelve Parts

## I

We've only just begun
Grasp the twisting mire of this history

On the road to criminal ancestry
A sheath gone wander

Expose the blade to human gully
Trenched by libations

Vital flow
Run thin

## II

Imesti
Jar with a head like mine

Hold the liver of a brother thieved
Qebehsenuef

Trade your contents for cash
Sudan's organs

Like blood diamond
Money for the caliphate war

## III

Lord, this yoke
This tailored refuse

We've tasted with our tongues
Driven with our spirits

Sung with our limbs
Resurrected with our eyes

Sequestered your tally and vowed
That deliverance will come

## IV

The bridges have been burned
Brethren

But we are also of water
And need not the passage

Born with fire on our tongues
We breathe our children's repose

Arrived in a place so strange
The trees lean wrong

## V

There is power in a single act
Resistance in a bearded man

A woman who walks this earth
Knowing her strength

And somewhere across the Atlantic
Bones – bones – bones

Covering the ocean floor
Like sand granules

## VI

No one speaks the story of the woman
Who cut her hair in pine

Let each strand go
Down river

No one tells the truth of the man
Who only dreamt to feed his children

Gave his dignity for bread
And entreated the sun for blindness

## VII

And their eyes still scourge us
Buried beneath our skin

Frayed like a fern leaf
We are torn between two lines

Migratory foot paths
Leading to a new haunt

Refugee tents where dreams are made
Hair parted by blood

## VIII

The minarets curve like dandelions
Uneasy in their own tendency

A bird of the sky, recluse in haze
Dots the horizon like satellite dishes

The men on their knees, aiming towards space
Touch concrete to root ground

Prayers take flight
And find their home in elevated ears

## IX

Young boys float
So as not to disturb the fallen

Feet suspended in air
The earth a graveyard

Soldiers for twisted desires
Troopers for power lust

They dream of balancing bread on their palms
Pedaling bicycles in a new direction

## X

Roadways skirt the farm
Too close to spire and mortar

Drag stalk to earth
Make bails in the shadow of bricks

Up river there is a tumbling
Down the bank like billowing smoke

Children live in liquid contour
Edfu and electrical towers

# XI

Race to grace the Nile
Salve from heat

Lily expanse in the crane's path
Island marsh, in the center of this river

One push from shore
One paddle to touch

Doum shade points
Haven in the right direction

# XII

East from here, Moses split the sea in two
In the country of waiting

Made the crag peaks into home
In the land of duality

Serket, stone-memory
Hold the rock as evidence

Make your children to feel their weight
Compass their spines towards rectitude

# Tainted Waters

we have crossed the corners
of geography
to find the aroma of home

frankincense & coffee
rising from its basin
to rally in the ethereal

skin etched
in the script of belief
a smoke rising from our eyes

we stand on the edge of this concrete blockade
& in love with language
make letters of golden symbols

birds of alabaster lined in the sand
ancient sentences pointing to a curved geography

symbols spelling fissure
the conjuring recede of a lake
named for evil

antecedents surface again
nilometer of vitals
glorious lacerations of sun
grace land and air
dry the clay of the water jug
expose the villages of indigo nights
and make their face to be shown
in the song of Napata

rejoice in this resurrection dance
and watch Nuba become whole once more

# Nile Procession

*for Hamza El Din (1929–2006)*

Never created ourselves
So praise be to the ancestors
Who show us wisdom
In the tantamount night

When the water line breaks from shore
Raise our heads to the subjugated flowering
Of the lotus that never closes

Keeps a reminder
Like your silence
Tells us you are where you should be
Brushing with the skin of a tree

If the bird of peace were to rise from earth's ashes
Could we hear her song
Like we hear yours?
Will the village rhythm match the beat
Of the donkey's click
Or have we only one song left to sing?

Your village was hung by the noose of modernity
Drowned her ancestral dust
To birth concrete & artificial light

How many pieces of Africa
Must be scattered & burned
Drowned & hung
Before the world can hear your songs?

You curved the aged wood of your oud
Into a never-ending Nile

Made your hands her cataracts
Elevated our inner ear

You sing Paremhat
From the green of your lungs
Each note a furrow
A wish
Placed in the agricultural tome
Of epic memory

# Silence Speaks

Moon drifts inside the commotion of its cornea
Shadow reflected on the Nile
Braided through voluble sky

A woman runs her fingers
On the still dust of night
Remembering her past

*Open your palms to the seeds of papyrus*
*Let them sprout your name into being*

*Songs of fire*
*Songs of sun*

When Anuket visits her dreams
She will weave fertility
Into the coils of her hair

Adorned with scarab amulets
These will not be the trinkets of tourists
Nor the discarded

*Oh, how they trade her for things*
*Make her to twist her body*
*For paper amnesia*

She will raise the wind from within her breast
And breathe the breath of Sehel
The scarab will spark her wisdom

*If anyone should do you harm*
*If anyone should squeeze you for jilt*
*Tell them: heat can ratify heat*

Shenu protection
Like the circle around the sun

Ancestor guidance
Plead our wish
Raise our heads
In song

*Everything we've seen has already been clean*
*Everything we've seen has already been clean*

But they continue their subjugation
Ignore the flowering of multitudes
Make haste of weighty past

*Rise the river, rise*
*Take with it all her dreams*
*And irrigate the soil with her song*

# Right To Return

*for all the Refugees*

the tar brushes earth
signals a hollow calling
of a rippling history

down the stolen streets
grandmother's house stands still
walls cold to the touch of her ghost intruders

tabla sings a painted catastrophe
lamenting water drops in the groves
of this reality

each tree a depiction of warrior strength
made to spiral past
into every child's shade

the cobblestone embraces diasporic feet
ancestral keys hang from traveler's necks
ringing in the swollen feet of return

summon the sumac
make the earth a zaatar mist
cloud the torture in her blessed scent

curl the hill towards sunrise
erect her stone foundation
& make her soil to swallow pain

the traveler's feet are shaped by grace
wrapped in the leather of memory
they preserve her almond softness

carried on elder prayers
always for the heart-sojourner
uttered towards sea

wished forth like a memorial cloud

*oh Jerusalem, oh Bethlehem*
*oh Nablus on the hill*
*oh Gaza by the sea*
*oh Mogadishu, New Orleans*
*oh Darfur, Aswan*
*oh Asyut, oh Toshka*
*oh Accra, Asmara*
*oh Basra, Berbera*

may God calm your loss & eruption
carry your apparition music
across seas
so that each of your children's ears
will return to your call

stranded in these separation barracks
made wanderers by rule & decree
centuries of nourish
made born for economic forage
foreign stepping in a wayward land

we learn to make our beds of distance
sleep on the dream of return
weave each step of the journey
so as never to lose
our ancestral thread

we trace the orange
ether of dusk
climb the open notes
tomorrow's song
a tribute to our past

on the tipped wings of a bird
gone east
made convex like night
we follow her arch
unto the disappeared horizon

# Glossary

**al-Qahira**; Arabic; Name for Cairo.

**al-Fayoum**; Arabic; Name of the largest oasis in Egypt.

**Aker**; Ancient Egyptian; Earth-god who was often depicted as a 'double sphinx,' two lions facing back to back. Aker was closely associated with the junction of east and west. The lions facing in each direction symbolize the journey of the sun through the underworld each night.

**Ansina**; Town on the eastern banks of the Nile in middle Egypt.

**Anubis**; Ancient Egyptian; Canine god of the dead. Closely associated with embalming and mummification.

**Anuket**; Ancient Egyptian; Goddess of the area around the first Nile cataract. Usually depicted as a woman with a papyrus scepter.

**Baramos**; Coptic; El Baramos monastery located in the desert of Wadi el Natrun, northwest of Cairo.

**Boza**; Fermented beverage made of millet said to have originated in Mesopotamia 8,000–9,000 years ago.

**Coptic Prayer**; Recited during the Coptic liturgy;

*Raise the Nile to its measures*
*According to Your grace*
*Give joy to the face of the earth*
*May its furrows be abundantly watered*
*Its fruits be plentiful*
*Prepare the land for sowing and harvesting…*

**Dayr al-Barsha**; Arabic; Coptic village on the eastern banks of the Nile in middle Egypt.

**Dijla**; Arabic; name for the Tigris River.

**Doum**; A type if palm tree native to the Nile river valley which bears edible fruits. In 2007 a team of Egyptian archeologists found eight baskets of 3,000 year old doum fruits in the tomb of Tutankhamen.

**Edfu**; Ancient Egyptian; Temple located in upper Egypt.

**Gallabiyya**; Egyptian Arabic; Tunic commonly worn in Egypt.

**Gebel Barkal**; Ancient Egyptian; literally "pure mountain"; located in Napata region.

**Ginn**; Egyptian Arabic; An intelligent spirit of lower rank than the angels, able to appear in human and animal forms and to possess humans.

**Hamza el Din**; (1929–2006) Nubian musician, composer, ethnomusicologist, and oud master.

**Hasad**; Arabic; Harvest.

**Horus**; Ancient Egyptian; god of the sky. Often depicted as a man with the head of a falcon, he symbolized the embodiment of the divine.

**Hudhud**; Arabic; The Hoopoe bird.

**Imesti**; Ancient Egyptian; God with a human head associated with the liver in the process of mummification. *

**Insan**; Arabic; Human being.

**Kamanga**; Arabic; Violin.

**Kom Ombo**; Ancient Egyptian; Temple located in upper Egypt.

**Kufiyah**; Arabic; Scarf.

**Mahmoud Darwish**; (1941–2008) Palestinian poet.

**Manetho**; (305–285 BC) Egyptian priest and historian from Tjebnutjer, an ancient city of Lower Egypt, later known as Sebennytos.

**Mubarak al-ati bism al-Rubb**; Arabic; "Blessed is he who comes in the name of the lord." From the Book of Psalms.

**Napata**; Ancient Egyptian; District of Nubia on the Dongola reach of the Nile near the fourth cataract.

**Nilometer**; A vertical surface serving to indicate the height to which the Nile rises during its annual floods.

**Nuba**; Arabic; Name for Nubia.

**Oud**; Arabic; A traditional short-necked lute.

**Papyrus of Ani**; Ancient Egyptian; Commonly known as the Ancient Egyptian Book of the Dead.

**Paremhat**; Coptic; The seventh month on the Coptic calendar occurring from early March to early April.

**Qebehsenuef**; Ancient Egyptian; God with a falcon head associated with the intestines in the process of mummification. *

**Ra**; Ancient Egyptian; Sun god. Often depicted as a man with the head of a hawk and a sun disc headdress. In the evolution of ancient Egyptian belief, Ra became the universal deity into which all other deities could be absorbed.

**Rekhyt**; Ancient Egyptian; Lapwing, a species of plover often depicted in Ancient Egyptian art with its wings pinned behind its back as a symbol of captivity.

**Scetis**; A part of the Egyptian desert south of Alexandria in the Wadi el Natrun valley.

**Sehel**; Ancient Egyptian; Island in the Nile where a temple for Anuket was built.

**Serket**; Ancient Egyptian; Goddess of protection represented with a rearing scorpion on her head. Her name is an abbreviation of *Serket Hetyt*, "The one who causes the throat to breathe."

**Shatan**; Arabic; Satan.

**Shenu**; Ancient Egyptian; Symbol of encircling protection, symbol of infinite.

**Sohag**; Governorate of Egypt along the Nile river in upper Egypt.

**Tabla**; Arabic; Common drum played in Egypt, traditionally made of clay with a goatskin head.

**Tar**; Arabic; Traditional single-frame drum made of wood with a goatskin head.

**Thebes**; Ancient Egyptian; It was considered the principle city of Upper Egypt in ancient Egyptian times.

**Zaatar**; Arabic; A specific mixture of herbs and spices.

**Zeytun**; Arabic; Olive. In this case it is a reference to a district in Cairo.

\* In Ancient Egyptian culture alabaster jars with differing heads were made to hold the contents of human remains after mummification.

# Acknowledgments

Sincere gratitude goes to the editors of the following journals and books where several of these pieces originally appeared in various forms:
America! What's My Name?: The Other Poets Unfurl the Flag; *The Baltimore Review*; *Black Renaissance/Renaissance Noire*; *Center for Middle Eastern Studies Online Magazine, Harvard University*; *Farafina Magazine*; *Five Fingers Review*; *From the Fishouse: An Audio Archive of Emerging Poets*; Inclined to Speak: Contemporary Arab American Poetry; *OCHO, Sou'wester Magazine*; Speaking for the Generation: New Writings from Africa; *To Topio: Poetry International*; *Warpland: Journal of Black Literature and Ideas*; *Zoland Poetry*.

Also, praise be where praise is due. This book would not have been possible without the support of: the Lannan Foundation for the much needed Marfa Residency, my incredible editors at BOA Editions for sharing in the love of this art, Amiri Baraka, A. Van Jordan, and Patricia Smith, for putting their stamp on it, Michael Wiegers for his bird's eye view and humor, Sherwin Bitsui for the long desert drives and consistent presence, Chris Abani for his inspiring brotherhood and unwavering grace, David St. John for his forthright vision and dedication, Antwi Akom for the daily reminders, Lemlem Rijio for all the nights of injera, Mahader Tesfai for the color and laughter, Suheir Hammad for lighting the way, Ahmed Ghappour for making the ultimate connection, John Carlos Perea for the familial soundtrack, Anthony and Maryann, Mama and Pops for setting the bar and insisting upon it, and all of my family, past and present.

## About the Author

Matthew Shenoda is the author of *Somewhere Else* (Coffee House Press), winner of the American Book Award. He currently lives in Los Angeles and is Assistant Provost for Equity & Diversity and Faculty in the School of Critical Studies at California Institute of the Arts. For more information visit: www.matthewshenoda.com

# BOA Editions, Ltd.

## AMERICAN POETS CONTINUUM SERIES

# Colophon

*Seasons of Lotus, Seasons of Bones*, by Matthew Shenoda is set in Cochin, designed by Georges Peignot in 1913. The typeface was based on Nicolas Cochin's eighteenth century engravings. In 1977, Matthew Carter expanded this historic form into a three part series.

———

The publication of this book is made possible, in part, by the following individuals:

Anonymous

Alan & Nancy Cameros

Bernadette Catalana

Gwen & Gary Conners

Peter & Suzanne Durant

Pete & Bev French

Judy & Dane Gordon

Kip & Debby Hale

Bob & Willy Hursh

Robin Hursh

Nora A. Jones

X. J. & Dorothy M. Kennedy

Laurie Kutchins

Rosemary & Lewis Lloyd

Elissa & Ernie Orlando

Boo Poulin

Deborah Ronnen & Sherman Levey

Paul & Andrea Rubery

Steven O. Russell & Phyllis Rifkin-Russell

Vicki & Richard Schwartz

Pat & Mike Wilder

Glenn & Helen William